Reasons for Christians to Celebrate the Biblical Feasts

And the LORD spake unto Moses, saying, Speak unto the children of Israel, and say unto them, Concerning the feasts of the LORD, which ye shall proclaim to be holy convocations, even these are my feasts.
Leviticus 23:1-2 KJV

Brenda and Dan Cathcart

Cover Design: by Dan Cathcart

ISBN: 978-1453763236
EAN-13: 9781453763230

Published by Moed Ministries, LLC

Office address:
3007 D Street SE
Auburn, WA 98002

Visit us on the web at www.moedministries.com

Visit our blog at www.moedtorah.blogspot.com

Table of Contents

Foreword

What are these strange holidays that the Jewish people celebrate? Did you know that God instituted them? We read in the Gospels that Jesus was crucified on the Passover, But what is the Passover? Is there any significance to the fact that Jesus died on Passover? What about the other "Jewish Feasts"? These feasts are Unleavened Bread, First Fruits and Feast of Weeks in the spring; Trumpets, Yom Kippur and Tabernacles in the fall. What are these feasts all about? Do they hold any significance in the life of Jesus and the lives of His Christian followers?

This collection of essays will answer these questions in a powerful way. The holidays we traditionally think of as Jewish holidays hold a great significance to the Bible believing Christian. The Feasts described first in the book of Leviticus chapter 23 are the embodiment of Messianic prophesies. The four spring feasts are all about Jesus' first coming. The three fall feasts are a "dress rehearsal" for His return and the millennial reign at the end of the age.

In Leviticus 23 verses 1 & 2 it says:

> And the LORD spoke to Moses, saying, Speak to the sons of Israel and say to them, The feasts of the LORD, which you shall proclaim, holy convocations, *even these are My appointed feasts.* (MKJV)

The important point here is that as the LORD, Yahweh, begins to describe the Feasts, He says that they are "My appointed feasts." He did not say "these are YOUR feasts," speaking to the Children of Israel, but that they are His feasts. They are for all who believe and call upon the name of the LORD. The Hebrew word in the original manuscripts of the Bible that is translated as "feast" is "moed." When we hear the word "feast" we generally think of food. But the word Moed means much more than eating. It literally means "appointed time." The word translated convocation is the Hebrew word "migra" which also means a "dress rehearsal." The feasts are God's divine appointments with His people. They are dress rehearsals pointing to the redemption of man and a reestablishment of His kingdom here on Earth.

In these essays, you will find a brief overview of the Biblical Feasts and discover why they are significant to you as a Christian believer. They will give you reasons to incorporate them into your life and enrich your understanding and relationship to God the Father, who gave us the feasts and to His son Jesus who is the embodiment of the word of God. We have included reasons to celebrate the feasts of Purim and Hanukkah as well. The book of Esther establishes the celebration of Purim, and the gospel of John tells us that Jesus celebrated Hanukkah. Like the other feasts, Purim and Hanukkah have historical, spiritual and prophetic significance.

It is our prayer that you will enjoy these essays as much as we enjoyed writing them. We pray that you will begin to understand the powerful message contained in the feasts, the "divine appointments" that the LORD gave us all so that we may meet Him and fellowship with Him. May the LORD richly bless you and your family.

Dan & Brenda Cathcart

Passover

In the fourteenth day of the first month, between the evenings, is the LORD's Passover,

(Leviticus 23:5 MKJV)

Reason One for Christians to Celebrate Passover:
The Bread

Luke 22:19-20 NKJV And He took bread, gave thanks and broke it, and gave it to them, saying, "This is My body which is given for you; do this in remembrance of Me." Likewise He also took the cup after supper, saying, "This cup is the new covenant in My blood, which is shed for you.

This passage is very familiar to Christians. We read these words of Jesus every time we have communion. But what bread and what cup is Jesus talking about? Luke tells us that this is a Passover meal in Luke 22:13-14. The bread Jesus is talking about is a specific piece of bread that is eaten at a specific time in the Passover Seder or order of service.

First, this bread is matzah or unleavened bread representing the absence of decay. Decay comes from death which we know originally comes from sin, specifically the sin of Adam (Romans 5:14). The Passover meal institutes the Feast of Unleavened bread which begins at sunset as the Passover meal is being eaten. The Israelites were to eat only unleavened bread during this seven day Feast of Unleavened Bread. In fact, they were to search out their houses and remove all the leaven. Unleavened bread does not decay or mold. It is like a package of soda crackers; it can sit in your cupboard for years and not get moldy. As such, it has the opposite effect from that of sin which leads to death and decay. David prophesies in Psalm 16:10 that God would not suffer His Holy One to see decay referring to Jesus' death and resurrection before His body could decay. Paul tells us that leavening represents sin as he refers to the unleavened bread of Passover.

> 1 Corinthians 5:6-7 NKJV Your glorying is not good. Do you not know that a little leaven leavens the whole lump? Therefore purge out the old leaven, that you may be a new lump, since you truly are unleavened. For indeed Christ, our Passover, was sacrificed for us.

Paul goes on to say that those who eat unworthily of this bread, who harbor sin in their lives, will be prone to sickness and early death (1Cor. 11:27-30).

Second, the bread is called the bread of affliction in remembrance of the affliction of their slavery in Egypt.

> Deuteronomy 16:3 NKJV "You shall eat no leavened bread with it; seven days you shall eat unleavened bread with it, that is, the bread of affliction (for you came out of the land of Egypt in haste), that you may remember the day in which you came out of the land of Egypt all the days of your life.

As the Passover Seder progresses, Jesus dips a piece of the bread of affliction into bitter herbs and gives it to Judas Iscariot the one who would betray him (John 13:26). Judas would taste the bitterness of condemnation and would later hang himself. Jesus would experience the bitterness of betrayal. But after the bitterness comes redemption.

Later in the meal, a different piece of unleavened bread is eaten. Before the Seder begins, there are three pieces of unleavened bread set aside in a special holder. After the

Seder begins, the middle piece of bread is removed, two-thirds of it broken off, wrapped in linen and hidden away. After the meal is finished, the children seek and find this hidden piece of bread called the afikomen or "that which comes after." It is this piece of bread that Jesus says represents His body and is broken for them. Jesus' body was broken, wrapped in linen and hidden away in the grave. After three days, He rose from the dead and those who eat of the bread He gives them will have eternal life.

John 6:51 NKJV "I am the living bread which came down from heaven. If anyone eats of this bread, he will live forever; and the bread that I shall give is My flesh, which I shall give for the life of the world."

Christians can celebrate Passover to remember His body that is broken for us.

Reason Two for Christians to Celebrate Passover:
The Cup

Luke 22:19-20 NKJV And He took bread, gave thanks and broke it, and gave it to them, saying, "This is My body which is given for you; do this in remembrance of Me." Likewise He also took the cup after supper, saying, "This cup is the new covenant in My blood, which is shed for you.

In this passage, Jesus is referring to a specific cup drank during the Passover Seder or order of service. This cup is actually the third cup. There are four cups of wine served at a Passover Seder, each with a meaning from Exodus 6:6-7.

"Therefore say to the children of Israel:
1) 'I am the LORD; I will bring you out from under the burdens of the Egyptians,
2) I will rescue you from their bondage, and
3) I will redeem you with an outstretched arm and with great judgments.
4) 'I will take you as My people, and I will be your God. Then you shall know that I am the LORD your God who brings you out from under the burdens of the Egyptians.

The first cup is the cup of sanctification setting His people aside for Him.

Exodus 2:24 NKJV So God heard their groaning, and God remembered His covenant with Abraham, with Isaac, and with Jacob.

Peter tells us that we are set aside for God.

1 Peter 2:9 MKJV But you are a chosen generation, a royal priesthood, a holy nation, a people for possession, so that you might speak of the praises of Him who has called you out of darkness into His marvelous light;

The second cup is the cup of deliverance breaking the chains that hold them to Egypt. He sets them free from slavery.

John 8:34-36 NKJV Jesus answered them, "Most assuredly, I say to you, whoever commits sin is a slave of sin." And a slave does not abide in the house forever, but a son abides forever. "Therefore if the Son makes you free, you shall be free indeed.

The third cup is the cup of redemption. It is this cup that Jesus says is the new covenant in His blood. Moses said that God brought them out of Egypt with great judgments, signs and wonders. Peter says that we are bought with the blood of Jesus which is more precious than any earthly wealth.

1 Peter 1:18-19 NKJV knowing that you were not redeemed with corruptible things, like silver or gold, from your aimless conduct received by tradition from your fathers, but with the precious blood of Christ, as of a lamb without blemish and without spot.

The fourth cup is the cup of acceptance or hope. Jesus did not drink of this cup. He said that He would drink it again with them in His kingdom.

Mark 14:25-26 NKJV "Assuredly, I say to you, I will no longer drink of the fruit of the vine until that day when I drink it new in the kingdom of God." And when they had sung a hymn, they went out to the Mount of Olives.

We, however, can drink the fourth cup in anticipation of His return. He promises us that He will come again and that where He is we will be also.

So, we can celebrate the Passover and as we drink of the cups, we can remember that we are set aside for God, the God who keeps His covenant for thousands of generations. We can remember that we are set free from the slavery of the flesh that leads to sin and death. We can remember that Jesus paid our price that we could not pay. And we can anticipate that He is coming again and He will take us as His people.

Revelation 22:7 NKJV "Behold, I am coming quickly! Blessed is he who keeps the words of the prophecy of this book."

Reason Three to Celebrate Passover

When we talk about celebrating Passover, we think of the Passover meal or Seder. The Passover meal is the time when the story of the Exodus is told. It is the story of God remembering His covenant with Abraham, Isaac and Jacob. It is the story of God's judgment on the gods of Egypt. It is the story of God's redemption. It is the story of the Patriarch Joseph's empty grave. It is the story of crossing the Red Sea. The story told at Passover began before the actual day of Passover and extended until the Israelites safely crossed the Red Sea.

Likewise the observance of Passover begins days before the actual Passover Seder. In fact, the Passover meal or Seder is the last thing that happens on the day of Passover. Jesus celebrated His final Passover with His disciples one day early, though. He knew that on the actual day of Passover, He would be the Passover lamb for the world. He celebrated the Passover Seder early to pass on instructions to the disciples about the changed but continued observance of the events of Passover. In fact, the observance of His last Passover Seder wasn't the most important event of those days, but it pointed to those events. What are those events leading up to Passover?

Before Passover those observing the Passover chose a lamb. They examined the lamb carefully to be sure it was without blemish. The Hebrew word for the phrase without blemish is tamiym which also refers to a morally upright character. Jesus presented Himself to the temple on the fourth day before Passover. He submitted to the questions of the

Pharisees, Sadduccess, Scribes and Herodians. They all questioned Him and could find no fault with Him.

Before the Passover begins, everyone had to clean out their houses and make sure there was no leaven fulfilling the commandment that there is to be no leaven in the camp during the Feast of Unleavened Bread. Jesus cleaned His house as well. He went to the temple, the house of His Father, and cleaned house by driving out the crooked moneylenders and merchants who cheated the pilgrims who came up to Jerusalem for the Feast.

The Passover lambs had to be bound to a stake, taken before the altar and slain. The priests caught the blood and poured it out at the foot of the altar. This all began at 9:00 a.m. or the third hour. Jesus was bound to His stake at the third hour. The sacrifices went on all day long until the hour of the evening sacrifice at the ninth hour or 3:00 p.m. At that time, the high priest slays the last Passover lamb and states, "It is finished." On that Particular Passover, darkness covered the land from the sixth until the ninth hour. At the ninth hour, Jesus cried out, "It is finished," and yielded up His spirit.

At His last Passover meal, Jesus gave instructions to remember Him during this meal that is all about remembrance. Like the story of the Exodus, the telling doesn't stop with the slaying of the Passover Lamb; it continues into the days following. It continues through His burial as the Feast of Unleavened bread begins. It continues three days later when He rose from the dead which just happened in that year to be on the Feast of Firstfruits.

We can observe the Passover by telling this story. Telling the story of the Passover of Jesus' death which just happened to parallel exactly the events at the temple. Telling the story of His burial as the Feast of Unleavened Bread begins. Telling the story of His resurrection on the Feast of Firstfruits. Telling the story of the Promise of our own glorified bodies represented by the seven days of the Feast of Unleavened Bread. We can tell the story of the first redemption out of Egypt and let it add meaning and significance to the second redemption from sin and death as we go through the Passover Seder.

Let's not diminish His sacrifice by failing to recognize all the prophecies fulfilled in those days. Our God is great and mighty doing marvelous works. Let's proclaim them all!

> Psalms 118:26-29 NKJV Blessed is he who comes in the name of the LORD! We have blessed you from the house of the LORD. God is the LORD, And He has given us light; Bind the sacrifice with cords to the horns of the altar. You are my God, and I will praise You; You are my God, I will exalt You. Oh, give thanks to the LORD, for He is good! For His mercy endures forever.

Unleavened Bread

...and on the fifteenth day of the same month is the Feast of Unleavened Bread to the LORD. You must eat unleavened bread seven days.

(Leviticus 23:6 MKJV)

Reason One to Celebrate the Feast of Unleavened Bread

The Feast of Unleavened Bread is a seven day Feast which begins at sunset as the day of Passover ends. In the Bible, the new day begins at sunset. In Genesis chapter one, during the creation story, we are told that "the evening and morning" make up one day. So, God has us start each day in darkness and He brings light into it.

The beginning of the Feast of Unleavened Bread is important because of its prophetic significance. Jesus died on Passover at 3:00 in the afternoon and was buried quickly because the Sabbath was coming! John calls this Sabbath a High Sabbath.

> John 19:31 NKJV Therefore, because it was the Preparation Day, that the bodies should not remain on the cross on the Sabbath (for that Sabbath was a high day), the Jews asked Pilate that their legs might be broken, and that they might be taken away.

A High Sabbath is a day in a Feast of the LORD that God commanded to be observed as a Sabbath whether the actual day of the week is a Saturday or not. The first and last days of the Feast of Unleavened Bread are High Sabbaths.

But what is the significance of unleavened bread? As we mentioned in our "Reasons to Celebrate Passover," bread that is unleavened does not decay. This theme of being resistant to decay is seen throughout the construction of the Tabernacle and in the offerings themselves. The wood used in the Tabernacle is acacia wood which hardens when dried and doesn't easily rot especially when overlaid with gold or bronze. The sacrifices themselves are offered with salt which is a preservative.

When Adam sinned, death entered the world. Everything that dies decays. But Paul tells us that although death entered through Adam, life comes through Jesus.

> Romans 5:17 NKJV For if by the one man's offense death reigned through the one, much more those who receive abundance of grace and of the gift of righteousness will reign in life through the One, Jesus Christ.

So, as Jesus is laid in the tomb, the Feast of Unleavened Bread is about to begin. The promise of resurrection is present in the very hour of His burial! As Peter said in his quote of Psalm 16:10, Jesus' body would not see decay but would be resurrected. His resurrection is on the third day of the Feast of Unleavened Bread. He is the firstfruits of the resurrection.

If Jesus rose on the third day and the Feast of Unleavened Bread is about the promise of His resurrection, then why does the Feast last seven days? Both the numbers three and seven are important in the Bible. Three is the number of divine completion; it is fitting that Jesus rose on the third day. Seven is the number of spiritual completion. It looks forward to the completion of all things. Paul tells us that Jesus is the Firstfruits, but we also have part in the resurrection to come. The seven days is the promise that we will also have new bodies that will not decay.

1 Corinthians 15:20-23 NKJV But now Christ is risen from the dead, and has become the firstfruits of those who have fallen asleep. For since by man came death, by Man also came the resurrection of the dead. For as in Adam all die, even so in Christ all shall be made alive. But each one in his own order: Christ the firstfruits, afterward those who are Christ's at His coming.

We can celebrate the Feast of Unleavened Bread in rejoicing that Jesus is risen from the grave and in anticipation that we also will be resurrected.

Reason Two to Celebrate the Feast of Unleavened Bread

Jesus said in His last Passover Seder that the bread of the Passover represented His body. Moses, in the book of Deuteronomy, calls the unleavened bread the bread of affliction.

> Deuteronomy 16:3 NKJV "You shall eat no leavened bread with it; seven days you shall eat unleavened bread with it, that is, the bread of affliction (for you came out of the land of Egypt in haste), that you may remember the day in which you came out of the land of Egypt all the days of your life.

As we look at the unleavened bread, we see that it is striped from the racks on which it is baked quickly at a high temperature and pierced to bake evenly. The result is a picture of Jesus' final Passover day when He was striped with the whips of the Roman soldiers and His side pierced to hasten His death, or so the Roman soldier thought but Jesus was already dead. This gives added meaning to the very familiar passage in Isaiah.

> Isaiah 53:5-6 NKJV But He was wounded for our transgressions, He was bruised for our iniquities; The chastisement for our peace was upon Him, And by His stripes we are healed. All we like sheep have gone astray; We have turned, every one, to his own way; And the LORD has laid on Him the iniquity of us all.

He paid the penalty for our iniquities by the suffering of His own body. He willingly paid this price because of the love He has for each and every one of us. In turn, we are called to present our bodies as a living sacrifice.

Romans 12:1-2 KJV I beseech you therefore, brethren, by the mercies of God, that ye present your bodies a living sacrifice, holy, acceptable unto God, which is your reasonable service. And be not conformed to this world: but be ye transformed by the renewing of your mind, that ye may prove what is that good, and acceptable, and perfect, will of God.

An offering to God cannot have any leaven in it. Part of the commandment to observe the Feast of Unleavened bread is to remove all the leaven from the house and even from the community. Paul tells us in 1 Corinthians 5 that leaven represents sin. He urges the Corinthians to purge out the leaven and keep the Feast with the unleavened bread of sincerity and truth.

A Jewish custom on the eve of the Passover after all the leaven is removed from the house is to hide a small bit of leaven somewhere in the house. The children of the house search for the bit of leaven as the father lights their way with a candle. When they find the leaven, the father warns them not to touch it. Instead the father uses a feather to sweep the leaven onto a wooden spoon which he then wraps in a linen cloth. The father takes the leaven on the spoon wrapped in the cloth outside the home to a community bonfire where the leaven from all the homes is burned.

In this custom, we can see a metaphor for God removing the leaven from our lives. He guides us with the Holy Spirit to identify the areas in our lives where we have fallen short. He warns us not to touch it, but to let Him deal with it. He carefully and fully sweeps the leaven onto the wooden cross of Jesus' death, wraps it in the linen of His burial shroud and takes it fully and completely out of our lives. What is burned away cannot be taken back.

The Feast of Unleavened Bread is a time to physically give up leavened bread to remind us that Jesus took on His body the penalty for all our sins redeeming us to eternal life. It reminds us to examine our lives and let the Holy Spirit show us where we need to allow God to work in our lives. It is also a time to pray that God would bring us together as a community and show us where the community as a whole needs to allow God's cleansing work.

Psalm 139 is a wonderful Psalm to meditate on during this Feast. Its closing words are a prayer I encourage all of you to pray.

> Psalms 139:23-24 KJV Search me, O God, and know my heart: try me, and know my thoughts: And see if there be any wicked way in me, and lead me in the way everlasting.

Feast of Firstfruits

And he shall wave the sheaf before the LORD to be received for you. On the next day after the sabbath the priest shall wave it.

(Leviticus 23:11 MKJV)

Reasons for Christians to Celebrate the Feast of Firstfruits

The Feast of Firstfruits falls during the week of the Feast of Unleavened Bread.

> Leviticus 23:10-11 NKJV "Speak to the children of Israel, and say to them: 'When you come into the land which I give to you, and reap its harvest, then you shall bring a sheaf of the firstfruits of your harvest to the priest. 'He shall wave the sheaf before the LORD, to be accepted on your behalf; on the day after the Sabbath the priest shall wave it.

The Feast of Firstfruits is observed on the "day after the Sabbath" during the Feast of Unleavened Bread. Since there are three Sabbaths during the Feast of Unleavened Bread, the regular weekly Sabbath, and the two end days celebrated as Sabbaths, it is not clear which day the scriptures mean. In 30 A.D., the year that Jesus died, two of these Sabbaths fell back to back and so the Feast of Firstfruits was on a Sunday. Passover was on a Thursday; the first day of the Feast of Unleavened Bread which is a High Sabbath was on a Friday. The weekly Sabbath is of course on Saturday and the Feast of Firstfruits fell on a Sunday. I think you are probably beginning to see that Jesus rose from the grave on the Feast of Firstfruits.

You are probably thinking that this day is not the Feast of Firstfruits but Easter! Well, you are half right. The Feast of Firstfruits is the name that God gave the day and the Israelites celebrated it for 1500 years before Jesus came.

24

Constantine renamed the feast more than 300 years after Jesus' resurrection. So for 300 years, Believers celebrated the Feast of Firstfruits! Christians today can celebrate the Feast of Firstfruits returning the original name to the day Jesus rose from the grave.

The name and the rituals surrounding the feast all point to Jesus' resurrection. In Jesus' day, the priests would begin preparing for the Feast of Firstfruits early on the 14th day of the first month, that is, the day of the Passover. The priests would go to a barley field near Jerusalem and tie up a bundle of barley that they would harvest as soon as the High Sabbath of the 15th was over at sundown. Or if the weekly Sabbath followed the High Sabbath, they would harvest it as soon as the Sabbath ended at sundown. That very night, they would thresh, roast and grind the grain into fine flour. As the first day of the week dawned, the ceremonies began. The people of Israel who had come to Jerusalem for this week of Feasts would bring their newly harvested sheaves of barley and their firstfruit offerings to the Temple. The priests would go out to meet them, take some of the sheaves, lift them into the air and wave them in all directions. They proceeded to the Temple with music, praise psalms, and dancing. The priests would then take the freshly ground flour, add frankincense and oil, and offer it on the altar along with a single lamb.

Now, correlate this with Jesus' death and resurrection. On the day of His death, early in the morning when He was bound to the cross, the priests tied the sheaf of barley and got it ready for harvest. On the days before His crucifixion, Jesus compared Himself to a kernel of grain.

> John 12:23-24 NKJV But Jesus answered them, saying, "The hour has come that the Son of Man

should be glorified. "Most assuredly, I say to you, unless a grain of wheat falls into the ground and dies, it remains alone; but if it dies, it produces much grain.

Then further in the chapter, Jesus says:
John 12:32 NKJV 32 "And I, if I am lifted up from the earth, will draw all peoples to Myself."

Jesus died and rose again being lifted up like the sheaf of barley. Grain planted in the earth grows and produces more grain. Jesus, being planted in the earth, produced a bountiful harvest. This also applies to us; we need to die with Jesus and be resurrected to new life.

Romans 6:4 NKJV Therefore we were buried with Him through baptism into death, that just as Christ was raised from the dead by the glory of the Father, even so we also should walk in newness of life.

After the priests lift up the sheaf, they offer the newly made grain on the altar. It symbolically rises to God in the smoke from the altar. It is an offering of Firstfruits. Jesus also went and presented Himself to God as the Firstfruits. Early in the morning of His resurrection, He appeared to Mary Magdalene but told her not to touch Him.

John 20:17 NKJV Jesus said to her, "Do not cling to Me, for I have not yet ascended to My Father; but go to My brethren and say to them, 'I am ascending to My Father and your Father, and to My God and your God.'"

Her message to the disciples was that Jesus was ascending to the Father. Paul calls Jesus the Firstfruits of the resurrection.

> 1 Corinthians 15:20 NKJV But now Christ is risen from the dead, and has become the firstfruits of those who have fallen asleep.

Jesus then returns and appears before the disciples encouraging them to touch Him and verify that He is Jesus returned in His glorified body.

> John 20:19-20 NKJV Then, the same day at evening, being the first day of the week, when the doors were shut where the disciples were assembled, for fear of the Jews, Jesus came and stood in the midst, and said to them, "Peace be with you." When He had said this, He showed them His hands and His side. Then the disciples were glad when they saw the Lord.

Christians already celebrate the Feast of Firstfruits. Next year when you are celebrating Jesus' resurrection, remember the actual name of the feast and all the prophetic events surrounding His resurrection. You see, God chose this day for the resurrection of His son before the foundation of the world. He chose the events of this day to be a rehearsal of His resurrection year after year until finally the actual year arrived. Now after His resurrection, we can observe these events and remember that He is the Firstfruits and that this is His feast named specially for Him.

Reasons for Christians to Count the Omer

When God gives the Israelites instructions for observing His feasts, he tells them to count the days from the Feast of Firstfruits to the Feast of Weeks.

> Leviticus 23:15-16 NKJV And you shall count for yourselves from the day after the Sabbath, from the day that you brought the sheaf of the wave offering: seven Sabbaths shall be completed. Count fifty days to the day after the seventh Sabbath; then you shall offer a new grain offering to the LORD.

Deuteronomy calls this day of the new grain offering the Feast of Weeks. The seventh Sabbath would be day forty-nine and the next day, the fiftieth day is the Feast Day.

> Deuteronomy 16:9-10 NKJV "You shall count seven weeks for yourself; begin to count the seven weeks from the time you begin to put the sickle to the grain. "Then you shall keep the Feast of Weeks to the LORD your God with the tribute of a freewill offering from your hand, which you shall give as the LORD your God blesses you.

The New Testament uses the Greek word Pentecost meaning fiftieth to describe the Feast. The countdown is actually a count up starting with one on the Feast of Firstfruits and concluding with fifty on the Feast of Weeks. The Jewish people call this period the Counting of the Omer. The Hebrew word Omer means sheaf. Literally, we are talking about sheaves of grain. Metaphorically, we are talking about the harvest of people. In Genesis 37, Joseph has a dream in which the sheaves of his brothers bow down to his sheaf establishing the precedent of sheaves representing people. Jesus represents the very first sheaf of barley harvested specifically for the Feast of Firstfruits. Paul calls him the firstfruits of the resurrection.

> 1 Corinthians 15:20 KJV But now is Christ risen from the dead, and become the firstfruits of them that slept.

We can think of the counting of the Omer as counting the sheaves that will be harvested. On the Feast of Weeks when the Holy Spirit falls, the harvest of those sheaves begins. On that day alone, three thousand people believed.

> Acts 2:41 KJV Then they that gladly received his word were baptized: and the same day there were added unto them about three thousand souls.

Although no one has yet fully attained the promise of the resurrection, the Holy Spirit is our down payment.

> Ephesians 1:13-14 NKJV In Him you also trusted, after you heard the word of truth, the gospel of your salvation; in whom also, having believed, you were sealed with the Holy Spirit of promise, who is the guarantee of our inheritance until the redemption of the purchased possession, to the praise of His glory.

Christians can participate in Counting the Omer by preparing ourselves anew for a renewing of the gift of the Holy Spirit who gives us power to accomplish the harvest of souls. Peter and the apostles were preparing themselves for this gift. After Jesus ascended into heaven, the apostles returned to Jerusalem where they appointed a man to replace Judas.

> Acts 1:21-22 NKJV "Therefore, of these men who have accompanied us all the time that the Lord Jesus went in and out among us, "beginning from the baptism of John to that day when He was taken up from us, **one of these must become a witness with us of His resurrection.**"

Peter was getting ready to receive the gift that Jesus told them to expect. He, along with all the apostles, was getting ready to witness to Jesus' resurrection because Jesus told them that they would be witnesses!

> John 15:26-27 NKJV "But when the Helper comes, whom I shall send to you from the Father, the Spirit of truth who proceeds from the Father, He will testify of Me. "And **you also will bear witness, because you have been with Me from the beginning**.

We can spend the time like the disciples did, in study and prayer, preparing ourselves to witness to Jesus' resurrection.

Feast of Weeks
(Pentecost)

And you shall count to you from the next day after the sabbath, from the day that you brought the sheaf of the wave offering; seven sabbaths shall be complete. To the next day after the seventh sabbath you shall number fifty days. And you shall offer a new food offering to the LORD.

(Leviticus 23:15-16 MKJV)

Reasons to Celebrate the Feast of Weeks

The spring Feasts of the LORD are all prophetic of Jesus' first coming. At Passover, Jesus died on the cross. Jesus' body was placed in the tomb as the seven day Feast of Unleavened Bread began. He rose from that tomb on the Feast of Firstfruits. The events of His First Coming culminate at the Feast of Weeks with the disciples receiving the gift of the Holy Spirit. We've all read the account of that day in the second chapter of the book of Acts, but in order to see the full impact of that day on the disciples and all who witnessed the events, we have to put the Feast into its historical perspective.

First, the Feast of Weeks doesn't happen in isolation. It occurs fifty days after the Feast of Firstfruits and is connected to this feast through counting the days from one feast to the next. This is called the counting of the Omer.

> Leviticus 23:15-16 NKJV 'And you shall count for yourselves from the day after the Sabbath, from the day that you brought the sheaf of the wave offering: seven Sabbaths shall be completed. 'Count fifty days to the day after the seventh Sabbath; then you shall offer a new grain offering to the LORD.

On the very day of Jesus' resurrection, the counting of the Omer began. The day of Jesus' ascension was the fortieth day of the counting of the Omer. On the day of His ascension, Jesus tells them that they would receive the Holy Spirit very soon.

Acts 1:4-5 NKJV And being assembled together with them, He commanded them not to depart from Jerusalem, but to wait for the Promise of the Father, "which," He said, "you have heard from Me; "for John truly baptized with water, but you shall be baptized with the Holy Spirit not many days from now."

Jesus' disciples were excited about this prospect and spent the last ten days leading up to the Feast of Weeks in the temple praising God.

Luke 24:52-53 NKJV And they worshiped Him, and returned to Jerusalem with great joy, and were continually in the temple praising and blessing God. Amen.

Second, the Feast of Weeks is a pilgrimage feast. All males were to appear before the LORD three times a year and the Feast of Weeks was one of those feasts.

Deuteronomy 16:10 NKJV "Then you shall keep the Feast of Weeks to the LORD your God with the tribute of a freewill offering from your hand, which you shall give as the LORD your God blesses you.

There would be over two million people in Jerusalem for the Feast of Weeks. They would all be going to the temple to present their offerings to God. This includes the disciples who would have even more reason to bring offerings of thanks to God as well as the devout Jews who traveled from all parts of the Roman Empire for this feast. These festivities began at 9:00 a.m., the time of the morning sacrifice.

Third, God gave the Covenant at Mt. Sinai in full view of all the gathered people of Israel on the first Feast of Weeks after the Exodus from Egypt. Jesus told His disciples that the events that began at Passover were the beginning of the New Covenant written of by Jeremiah. Surely, the disciples would be expecting something to happen on the anniversary of the Covenant at Mt. Sinai.

> Luke 22:19-20 NKJV And He took bread, gave thanks and broke it, and gave it to them, saying, "This is My body which is given for you; do this in remembrance of Me." Likewise He also took the cup after supper, saying, "This cup is the new covenant in My blood, which is shed for you.

> Jeremiah 31:31-33 NKJV "Behold, the days are coming, says the LORD, when I will make a new covenant with the house of Israel and with the house of Judah- "not according to the covenant that I made with their fathers in the day that I took them by the hand to lead them out of the land of Egypt, My covenant which they broke, though I was a husband to them, says the LORD. "But this is the covenant that I will make with the house of Israel after those days, says the LORD: I will put My law in their minds, and write it on their hearts; and I will be their God, and they shall be My people.

The outpouring of the Holy Spirit on the Feast of Weeks recreated the events of Mt. Sinai ratifying the New Covenant.

The Midrash, which is a commentary on the Torah, the five books of Moses, gives further details of the events of the first Feast of Weeks at Mt. Sinai. The Midrash says that tongues of fire circled and touched all the people gathered at Mt. Sinai. It says that there were thunderings and lightnings plural because God's voice came in all seventy languages of the nations but only Israel answered and said, "All that the LORD has spoken we will do."

With this background, we see that the most likely place for the Holy Spirit to fall on the disciples was at the temple in full view of the gathered multitude. The word house used to describe the disciples' location on the Feast of Weeks is the Greek oykos which also means temple.

> Acts 2:1-6 NKJV When the Day of Pentecost had fully come, they were all with one accord in one place. And suddenly there came a sound from heaven, as of a rushing mighty wind, and it filled the whole house where they were sitting. Then there appeared to them divided tongues, as of fire, and one sat upon each of them. And they were all filled with the Holy Spirit and began to speak with other tongues, as the Spirit gave them utterance. And there were dwelling in Jerusalem Jews, devout men, from every nation under heaven. And when this sound occurred, the multitude came together, and were confused, because everyone heard them speak in his own language.

Peter stands up and begins to preach. As Jesus promised, the power of the Holy Spirit is on him to preach the good news to all people.

> Acts 1:8 NKJV "But you shall receive power when the Holy Spirit has come upon you; and you shall be witnesses to Me in Jerusalem, and in all Judea and Samaria, and to the end of the earth."

Christians can celebrate the Feast of Weeks as we remember the incredible outpouring of the Holy Spirit on the disciples, and we can rejoice that this gift is to us as well.

> Acts 2:38-39 NKJV Then Peter said to them, "Repent, and let every one of you be baptized in the name of Jesus Christ for the remission of sins; and you shall receive the gift of the Holy Spirit. "For the promise is to you and to your children, and to all who are afar off, as many as the Lord our God will call."

The Feast of Weeks is a time of a new grain offering to the LORD. It is the time of the wheat harvest. The harvest season in Israel has begun. When Jesus sent His disciples out two by two to spread the message of the kingdom of heaven, he sends them out with these words recorded by Luke.

> Luke 10:2 NKJV Then He said to them, "The harvest truly is great, but the laborers are few; therefore pray the Lord of the harvest to send out laborers into His harvest.

As we celebrate the Feast of Weeks, we can pray that God will send workers, including ourselves, into His harvest.

Feast of Trumpets

*Speak to the sons of Israel saying:
In the seventh month, in the first
day of the month, you shall have a
sabbath, a memorial summons, a
holy convocation.*

(Leviticus 23:24 MKJV)

Reason One to Celebrate the Feast of Trumpets

The Feast of Trumpets is the first of the fall feasts of the LORD spoken of in Leviticus chapter 23.

> Leviticus 23:1-2 And the LORD spoke to Moses, saying, Speak to the sons of Israel and say to them, The feasts of the LORD, which you shall proclaim, holy convocations, even these are My appointed feasts. (MKJV)

The Feast days belong to God. He says in this passage that they are "My appointed feasts." They are not just for the Jewish people to observe, but for all who call on the name of the God of Abraham, Isaac and Jacob.

The first day of the month of Tishrei which usually starts in September is the Feast of Trumpets. The Bible tells us that this day is to be a memorial of blowing trumpets or the shofar (Lev. 23:24). The shofar is a trumpet made of a ram's horn.

Like all the Feasts of the LORD, it is a Mo'ed, an appointed time, which is to be observed with a holy convocation. The Hebrew word for convocation is migra', which can also be translated as a dress rehearsal. The Feast of Trumpets is an appointed time for the rehearsal of the coming of our King. The Feast of Trumpets looks back to God as king and creator of the universe and forward to the crowning of Jesus as priest and king.

The Jewish sages tell us that one reason to blow the shofar is to remember that God is King. In fact, the Jewish people believe that Adam was created on this day which is why this is also the Jewish New Year (Rosh Hashanah). When we blow the shofar on the Feast of Trumpets, we re-enthrone God as King in our lives.

> Psalms 47:1-9 MKJV To the Chief Musician. A Psalm for the sons of Korah. Clap your hand, all you peoples; shout to God with the voice of triumph. For the LORD Most High is awesome, a great king over all the earth. He shall humble the peoples under us, and nations under our feet. He shall choose our inheritance for us, the majesty of Jacob whom He loved. Selah. God has gone up with a shout, the LORD with the sound of a trumpet. Sing praise to God, sing praise; sing praise to our King, sing praise. For God is King of all the earth; sing praises with understanding. God reigns over the nations, God sits on the throne of His holiness. The rulers of the peoples are gathered together, the people of the God of Abraham; for the shields of the earth are God's; He is lifted up on high.

In the kingdom of Judah, the kings were enthroned on the Feast of Trumpets to the sound of the shofars. The shofars will sound once again to enthrone a new King of Israel. Jesus son of David will take His throne. Zechariah spoke of that day calling him the BRANCH.

> Zechariah 6:11-13 MKJV And take silver and gold, and make crowns, and set them on the head of Joshua the son of Jehozadak, the high priest. And speak to him, saying, So speaks the LORD of hosts, saying, Behold the Man whose name is The

BRANCH! And He shall spring up out of His place, and He shall build the temple of the LORD. Even He shall build the temple of the LORD; and He shall bear the glory, and shall sit and rule on His throne. And He shall be a priest on His throne; and the counsel of peace shall be between them both.

The Feast of Trumpets is an appointed day to deliberately remember that God is the ultimate King and that His son Jesus is coming to rule and reign for one thousand years. Let's rehearse this joyful event together.

Reason Two to Celebrate the Feast of Trumpets

Another reason to blow the shofar on the Feast of Trumpets is to call the nation to repentance and to call on God to have mercy on His people.

God appointed Ezekiel as a watchman over the house of Israel. He was to warn them of their error and call them to repentance. If the watchman did not warn, he would be held accountable for those who were lost in their sins.

> Ezekiel 33:6 MKJV But if the watchman sees the sword coming, and does not blow the trumpet and the people are not warned; if the sword comes and takes any person from among them, he is taken away in his iniquity. But I will require his blood at the watchman's hand.

Starting one month before the Feast of Trumpets on the first of Elul begins a forty day time of repentance and return to God. It coincides with Moses' second forty days on Mt. Sinai during which he achieved the atonement for Israel's sin of worshiping the golden calf.

On the Feast of Trumpets, the shofar is blown one hundred times in a series of blasts consisting of three different sounds. The first is the tekia, a long blast of alarm; the second is the shavirim, three medium blasts of wailing. The last type is the teruah, nine short blasts like a broken sob. The alarm is sounded for the repentance, return, and mourning for sins committed.

Like John the Baptist called for the people to repent and return making the way for Jesus, we need to call for repentance and return to make the way for the return of Jesus.

> Matthew 3:1-3 MKJV In those days John the Baptist came preaching in the wilderness of Judea, and saying, Repent, for the kingdom of Heaven is at hand. For this is he who was spoken of by the prophet Isaiah, saying, "The voice of one crying in the wilderness: Prepare the way of the Lord, make His path straight."

Paul warns us Gentiles not be puffed up in our pride that we were grafted into Israel while many of the natural branches were cut off.

> Romans 11:21-22 MKJV For if God did not spare the natural branches, fear lest He also may not spare you either! Behold then the kindness, and the severity of God; on those having fallen, severity; but on you, kindness, if you continue in the kindness. Otherwise you also will be cut off.

He then goes on to call us to live holy lives as of a sacrifice dedicated entirely to God.

> Romans 12:1 MKJV I beseech you therefore, brothers, by the mercies of God to present your bodies a living sacrifice, holy, pleasing to God, which is your reasonable service.

The Feast of Trumpets is a call to remember God and to live lives that bring honor and glory to Him.

Matthew 5:14-16 MKJV You are the light of the world. A city that is set on a hill cannot be hidden. Nor do men light a lamp and put it under the grain-measure, but on a lampstand. And it gives light to all who are in the house. Let your light so shine before men that they may see your good works and glorify your Father who is in Heaven.

At the same time, the call of the shofar is a reminder to God to have mercy on his people; that by hearing the shofar God will be moved to leave the judgment seat and go to the seat of mercy. The shofar is made from the horn of a ram. When Abraham was told to sacrifice Isaac, a ram was provided as a substitute. It was held captive in the thicket by its horns.

Genesis 22:13 MKJV And Abraham lifted up his eyes, and looked. And, behold, a ram behind him was entangled in a thicket by its horns. And Abraham went and took the ram and offered it up for a burnt offering instead of his son.

According to Jewish tradition, blowing the shofar reminds God of His promise to Abraham that his seed would inherit the land. It reminds God of the mercy He showed Abraham by sending the ram in Isaac's place.

As believers, the shofar reminds God of Abraham's obedience even to the offering of his own son believing that even so, God would fulfill His promises through Isaac. The writer of Hebrews says in the faith chapter that Abraham believed God could resurrect Isaac.

Hebrews 11:17-19 MKJV By faith Abraham, being tested, offered up Isaac. And he who had received the promises offered up his only-begotten son, of whom it was said that in Isaac your Seed shall be called, concluding that God was able to raise him up, even from the dead, from where he even received him, in a figure.

Surely, when God hears the shofar, He will remember not only Abraham's obedience but Jesus' obedience in enduring the cross.

Hebrews 12:2 MKJV looking to Jesus the Author and Finisher of our faith, who for the joy that was set before Him endured the cross, despising the shame, and sat down at the right of the throne of God.

When we hear the shofar, we too, remember the ram that died in our place making a way for us to have eternal life.

John 3:16 MKJV For God so loved the world that He gave His only-begotten Son, that whoever believes in Him should not perish but have everlasting life.

As we gather together on the Feast of Trumpets and hear the shofar sound out our cry of mourning for all the ways we have fallen short, we have confidence that He hears our cries and forgives. We call on God to continue to have mercy on us and on our loved ones. It is a good time to pray for our unsaved loved ones and people around the world.

Reason Three to Celebrate the Feast of Trumpets

The sound of the shofar signals the beginning of the Day of the LORD.

> Joel 2:1-2 MKJV Blow a ram's horn in Zion, and sound an alarm in My holy mountain; let all the inhabitants of the land tremble. For the day of the LORD comes, for it is near at hand; a day of darkness and of gloominess, a day of clouds and of thick darkness, as the morning spread on the mountains; a great people and a strong people; there has not been ever the like, nor shall there ever be again, even to the years of many generations.

We learned earlier that the shofar calls God to have mercy. He doesn't want any to perish but would rather that they come to repentance, but those who won't heed the call of the shofar will eventually face judgment.

> Ezekiel 18:23 MKJV Do I actually delight in the death of the wicked? Says the Lord Jehovah. Is it not that he should turn from his ways and live?

Jesus speaks of that day calling it a day when the sun will be darkened and the moon will not give its light.

> Matthew 24:29 MKJV And immediately after the tribulation of those days, the sun shall be darkened and the moon shall not give her light, and the stars shall fall from the heaven, and the powers of the heavens shall be shaken.

Daniel chapter 7 describes the Day of Judgment. The books will be opened.

> Daniel 7:9-10 MKJV I watched until the thrones were thrown up, and the Ancient of Days sat, whose robe was white as snow, and the hair of His head like the pure wool. His throne was like flames of fire, and His wheels like burning fire. A stream of fire went out and came out from before Him. A thousand thousands served Him, and ten thousand times ten thousand stood before Him. The judgment was set, and the books were opened.

Remember, that this is a forty day season of repentance, starting with Elul 1, thirty days before the Feast of Trumpets. The final ten days from the Feast of Trumpets to the tenth of Tishrei are called the Days of Awe. And the tenth of Tishrei just happens to be Yom Kippur, the Day of Atonement. Jewish tradition says that the books of life and death are opened on the Feast of Trumpets to determine one's fate for the coming year. The sentence is pronounced on the Feast of Trumpets but God in His mercy leaves the books open until the Day of Atonement when they are sealed and judgment for life or death begins. So, the Days of Awe are days of intense spiritual introspection.

As believers, we know that our names are written in the Book of Life and we are sealed by the Holy Spirit.

> 2 Corinthians 1:21-22 NKJV Now He who establishes us with you in Christ and has anointed us is God, who also has sealed us and given us the Spirit in our hearts as a guarantee.

So, Daniel 7:10 is on the Feast of Trumpets and the books are still open. When the shofar blows we are reminded that God will not delay His judgment forever. He is the righteous judge and He sends His son to render judgment on the earth.

> Jeremiah 33:14-15 NKJV 'Behold, the days are coming,' says the LORD, 'that I will perform that good thing which I have promised to the house of Israel and to the house of Judah: 'In those days and at that time I will cause to grow up to David A Branch of righteousness; He shall execute judgment and righteousness in the earth.

When we celebrate the Feast of Trumpets, we look forward to the millennial reign of the Messiah when He will rule and the land will have peace.

Reason Four to Celebrate the Feast of Trumpets

The sound of the shofar will awaken the dead. The passage in Matthew that we looked at in reason three goes on to describe the gathering of the saints.

> Matthew 24:30-31 MKJV And then the sign of the Son of man shall appear in the heavens. And then all the tribes of the earth shall mourn, and they shall see the Son of man coming in the clouds of the heaven with power and great glory. And He shall send His angels with a great sound of a trumpet, and they shall gather His elect from the four winds, from one end of the heavens to the other.

Paul says that the dead will be resurrected at this time.

> 1 Thessalonians 4:16-17 MKJV For the Lord Himself shall descend from Heaven with a shout, with the voice of the archangel and with the trumpet of God. And the dead in Christ shall rise first. Then we who are alive and remain shall be caught up together with them in the clouds, to meet the Lord in the air. And so we shall ever be with the Lord.

Daniel says the resurrection occurs when the Books of Life are opened which we saw occurred on the Day of the LORD which begins at the Feast of Trumpets.

> Daniel 12:1-2 MKJV And at that time Michael shall stand up, the great ruler who stands for the sons of your people. And there shall be a time of trouble,

such as never was since there was a nation; until that time. And at that time your people shall be delivered, every one that shall be found written in the book. And many of those who sleep in the dust of the earth shall awake, some to everlasting life, and some to shame and everlasting contempt.

Paul tells us that the trumpet that awakens the dead will be the "last trumpet."

1 Corinthians 15:52 MKJV in a moment, in a glance of an eye, at the last trumpet. For a trumpet shall sound, and the dead shall be raised incorruptible, and we shall all be changed.

Remember the one hundred blasts of the shofar that are blown at the Feast of Trumpets? The last one is an extra long blast and is called the last trumpet!

When we hear the shofar on the Feast of Trumpets we look forward to the resurrection of the dead and being caught up with the LORD. We rejoice in the coming of our incorruptible bodies.

Reason Five to Celebrate the Feast of Trumpets

The sound of the shofar signals the coming of the bridegroom. Jesus compared His return to a bridegroom returning for his bride (Matt. 25:1-13).

In an ancient Hebrew wedding, the father arranged a marriage for his son. The betrothal was considered as binding as the marriage. After the betrothal, the son returned to his father's house where he would prepare a bridal chamber for himself and his bride. The father would supervise the work and when it was done according to his satisfaction, the father would tell the son to go get his bride. He would do so immediately and without warning, frequently in the middle of the night. The groom's attendants, called the friends of the groom, would run before him blowing the shofar and shouting, "The bridegroom comes." The bride was expected to be ready to meet him. Ready or not, he was coming.

Just before Jesus' crucifixion, he tells his disciples that He is leaving to "prepare a place for them."

> John 14:2-3 MKJV In My Father's house are many mansions; if it were not so, I would have told you. I go to prepare a place for you. And if I go and prepare a place for you, I will come again and receive you to Myself, so that where I am, you may be also.

John the Baptist spoke of his role as that of a friend of the groom.

John 3:28-29 MKJV You yourselves bear witness to me that I said, I am not the Christ, but that I am sent before Him. He who has the bride is the bridegroom, but the friend of the bridegroom who stands and hears him rejoices greatly because of the bridegroom's voice. Then my joy is fulfilled.

John's joy will be full when Jesus comes for His bride who has made herself ready.

Revelation 19:7-9 MKJV Let us be glad and rejoice and we will give glory to Him. For the marriage of the Lamb has come, and His wife has prepared herself. And to her was granted that she should be arrayed in fine linen, clean and white. For the fine linen is the righteousness of the saints. And he said to me, Write, Blessed are those who have been called to the marriage supper of the Lamb. And he said to me, These are the true sayings of God.

When we hear the shofar on the Feast of Trumpets, we look forward to the coming of our bridegroom. We are reminded to be like the wise virgins, ready and watching for His return.

The spring feasts were a rehearsal for Jesus' first coming. For 1500 years before Jesus' first coming, the Jewish people observed the Feasts. Then one year exactly on Passover Jesus died at the exact hour that the final Passover lamb was slain. As the high priest pronounced the completion of the Passover with the words, "It is finished," Jesus also proclaimed, "It is finished" (John 19:30, Mark 15:34-37). On the third day, as the high priest lifts the firstfruits of the barley harvest and waves it before the LORD, Jesus rose from the dead and presented himself to God as the firstfruits of the resurrection (Luke 24:21, 1 Cor. 15:20). Fifty days later, as the observant Jews from all the nations gathered once again in Jerusalem to observe the Feast of Weeks, a great thunder came from heaven just like it did 1500 years earlier at Mt. Sinai. According to Jewish tradition, God's voice spoke at that time in all the languages of the nations. When the Holy Spirit fell on the disciples, they spoke in all the languages of the nations (Acts 2:1-12). They were the firstfruits of the wheat harvest.

What about the fall feasts? They occur at the end of the harvest year, the last of the grapes are harvested and put into the winepress and the final wheat harvest is being completed. Jesus Himself compares His coming to the fall harvest.

> Matthew 13:38-43 NKJV "The field is the world, the good seeds are the sons of the kingdom, but the tares are the sons of the wicked one. "The enemy who sowed them is the devil, the harvest is the end of the age, and the reapers are the angels. "Therefore as the tares are gathered and burned in the fire, so it will be at the end of this age. "The Son of Man will send out His angels, and they will gather out of His kingdom all things that offend, and those who practice lawlessness, "and will cast them into the furnace of fire. There will be wailing and gnashing of teeth. "Then the righteous will shine forth as the sun in the kingdom of their Father. He who has ears to hear, let him hear!"

The fall feasts, then, are a rehearsal for His second coming. The Feast of Trumpets is the first feast of the fall. It starts with the loud blast of the shofar. Jesus' second coming is announced with the trumpet blast of God! Some year on the Feast of Trumpets, Jesus will come again gathering his saints both those alive and those who were dead for His coronation and wedding! The day of judgment will begin.

> Revelation 14:14-16 MKJV And I looked, and behold, a white cloud. And on the cloud sat one like the Son of man, having a golden crown on His head, and a sharp sickle in His hand. And another angel came out of the temple, crying in a great voice to Him sitting on the cloud, Thrust in Your sickle and reap, for the time has come for You to reap, for the harvest of the earth was dried. And He sitting on the cloud thrust in His sickle on the earth, and the earth was reaped.

We observe the Feast of Trumpets as a rehearsal for Jesus' second coming. Imagine yourself at a Feast of Trumpets service and, as the last blast of the one hundred blasts resonates, suddenly there is a louder, clearer, all encompassing blast that fills the air. You look up and there in a dark, rapidly moving cloud is Jesus. And even before the realization comes to you that now is the time, your feet are already off the ground and you are on your way to meet your King, your Bridegroom, your Lord.

Yom Kippur:
The Day of Atonement

Also, on the tenth of this seventh month, this is a day of atonement. It shall be a holy convocation to you. And you shall afflict your souls and offer a fire offering to the LORD.
(Leviticus 23:27 MKJV)

Reason One to Celebrate Yom Kippur

The Day of Atonement is the one day a year when the high priest could enter the Holy of Holies. He entered the Holy of Holies to make atonement for Himself and his fellow priests and for the nation of Israel.

It falls on the tenth of Tishrei, ten days from the beginning of the Feast of Trumpets. One of the reasons to blow the trumpets was to remind God to have mercy on His people. Now, on the Day of Atonement, that will be put to the test. Will God come down and "sit" on the mercy seat of the Ark of the Covenant in the Holy of Holies or will He instead bring judgment? The ten days leading up to the Day of Atonement are called the Days of Awe, reminding us of the awe in which we should hold God. They are intense days of spiritual introspection marked by reviewing one's actions of the past year. It leads to sorrow for wrongs done to God and others, and repentance leading one back to walking in God's ways.

On this day, God says that His people are to "afflict their souls."

> Leviticus 23:27 MKJV Also, on the tenth of this seventh month, this is a day of atonement. It shall be a holy convocation to you. And you shall afflict your souls and offer a fire offering to the LORD.

This is interpreted as a full twenty-four hour fast, putting aside the needs and desires of the flesh and focusing totally on the spiritual, seeking God with all one's heart.

As believers in Jesus as our Messiah, we know that we have attained mercy by His blood that He shed for us and that we are sealed for that final day of redemption.

> Ephesians 1:13-14 MKJV in whom also you, hearing the word of truth, the gospel of our salvation, in whom also believing, you were sealed with the Holy Spirit of promise, who is the earnest of our inheritance, to the redemption of the purchased possession, to the praise of His glory.

Paul goes on to remind us that we must continue in the faith.

> Colossians 1:21-23 MKJV And you, who were once alienated and enemies in your mind by wicked works, yet now He has reconciled in the body of His flesh through death, to present you holy and without blame, and without charge in His sight, if indeed you continue in the faith grounded and settled, and are not moved away from the hope of the gospel, which you have heard and which was proclaimed in all the creation under Heaven, of which I, Paul, became a minister…

What does it mean to be grounded and settled? In his letter to the Ephesians, Paul expands on this theme.

> Ephesians 4:30-32 MKJV And do not grieve the Holy Spirit of God, by whom you are sealed until the day of redemption. Let all bitterness and wrath and anger and tumult and evil speaking be put away from you, with all malice. And be kind to one another, tenderhearted, forgiving one another, even as God for Christ's sake has forgiven you.

On the Day of Atonement, Christians can also set aside the desires of the flesh and participate in the Fast. How was our walk this year? Have we grown in our knowledge of God, in our faith and good deeds? Have we walked in the power of the Holy Spirit and allowed God to transform us into the image of His son?

> Romans 12:2 MKJV And do not be conformed to this world, but be transformed by the renewing of your mind, in order to prove by you what is that good and pleasing and perfect will of God.

Reason Two to Celebrate Yom Kippur

One of the reasons to blow the shofar on the Feast of Trumpets was to remind God to have mercy on His people on Yom Kippur. God desires to have mercy on everyone. His desire is that the rebellious repent of their sins and turn to Him.

> Ezekiel 33:11 MKJV Say to them: As I live, says the Lord Jehovah, I have no pleasure in the death of the wicked, but rather that the wicked turn from his way and live. Turn, turn from your evil ways; for why will you die, O house of Israel?

Peter says that God holds back His time of judgment waiting for people to come to repentance.

> 2 Peter 3:9 MKJV The Lord is not slow concerning His promise, as some count slowness, but is long-suffering toward us, not willing that any of us should perish, but that all of us should come to repentance.

Right now, God chooses to remain on His mercy seat granting forgiveness to all who seek Him and believe in the atoning sacrifice of Jesus, the Messiah.

> Romans 10:9-10 MKJV Because if you confess the Lord Jesus, and believe in your heart that God has raised Him from the dead, you shall be saved. 10 For with the heart one believes unto righteousness, and with the mouth one confesses unto salvation.

But there will come a time when God will say, "It is time." As He brought judgment on Israel and Judah, He will bring judgment on the nations.

> Joel 3:12-14 MKJV Let the nations be awakened and come up to the valley of Jehoshaphat; for there I will sit to judge all the nations all around. Put in the sickle, for the harvest is ripe. Come, come down; for the press is full; the vats overflow, for their wickedness is great. Multitudes, multitudes in the valley of decision; for the day of the LORD is near in the valley of decision!

He will establish His name in Jerusalem and it shall be a holy city consecrated to God.

> Joel 3:16-17 MKJV The LORD shall also roar out of Zion and utter His voice from Jerusalem. And the heavens and the earth shall shake. But the LORD will be the hope of His people and the strength of the sons of Israel. So you shall know that I am the LORD your God dwelling in Zion, My holy mountain. And Jerusalem shall be a holy thing, and no aliens shall pass through her any more.

Christians can celebrate the Day of Atonement in fasting for friends and loved ones to come to repentance and to accept that Jesus died for their sins and rose triumphant from the grave.

The Feast of Tabernacles

Speak to the sons of Israel, saying, the fifteenth day of this seventh month shall be the Feast of Tabernacles for seven days to the LORD.

(Leviticus 23:34 MKJV)

Reason One to Celebrate the Feast of Tabernacles

The Feast of Tabernacles is the seventh and last Feast in the Feast cycle which began in the spring with Passover. The month of Passover is the first month on the religious or redemption calendar established when Moses brought the Israelites out of Egypt. The Feast of Tabernacles is in the seventh month and lasts for seven days. That's three sevens here. Seven is the number of spiritual completion and three is the number of divine completion. The Feast of Tabernacles is a rehearsal of the completion of God's divine plan of salvation. Let's see how God reveals this in the establishment of the feast.

> Leviticus 23:39-40 MKJV Also in the fifteenth day of the seventh month, when you have gathered in the fruit of the land, you shall keep a feast to the LORD seven days. On the first day shall be a sabbath, and on the eighth day shall be a sabbath. And you shall take the fruit of majestic trees for yourselves on the first day, branches of palm trees, and the boughs of thick trees, and willows of the brook. And you shall rejoice before the LORD your God seven days.

The Jewish people use the branches of the palm, willow, and myrtle along with the citron which together are called a lulav to show rejoicing before God. The Jewish sages say this is in recognition that God is the Creator. He can be seen in the works of creation (Rom. 1:19-20) and creation itself worships God (Ps. 19:1, Hab. 2:14, Luke 19:37-40). As we rejoice before the LORD during the Feast of Tabernacles, we look forward to when "every knee will bow and every tongue confess that Jesus is LORD" (Phil. 2:11).

Isaiah says that all creation will burst out in praise when God finishes His plan for redemption.

> Isaiah 44:23 MKJV Sing, O heavens; for the LORD has done it. Shout, lower parts of the earth. Break out into singing, O mountains, O forest, and every tree in it. For the LORD has redeemed Jacob, and glorified Himself in Israel.

The observance of the feast manifests itself in the Israelites living in booths, tents or huts so that they will remember that God had them live in booths when they were brought out of Egypt.

> Lev. 23:41-44 MKJV And you shall keep it a feast to the LORD seven days in the year. It shall be a statute forever in your generations. You shall keep it in the seventh month. You shall live in booths seven days. All that are born Israelites shall live in booths, so that your generations may know that I made the sons of Israel live in booths when I brought them out of the land of Egypt. I am the LORD your God. And Moses declared the feasts of the LORD to the sons of Israel.

Again, the Israelites left the trappings of civilization and lived close to nature observing God in all their surroundings. But what was there about their time in the wilderness that should be brought to mind?

First, this was a time when God miraculously provided for all their needs. Manna rained down from heaven, water flowed out from a rock, and their clothing did not wear out. During the millennial reign of the Messiah, the ground of Israel will produce bountiful food (Jer. 31:12-14). Rain will be provided for all those who come up to Jerusalem to worship God during the Feast of Tabernacles (Zec. 14:16-18). After the thousand years, God will recreate the heavens and earth, and the tree of life will grow on both sides of the river of life. It will bear fruit each month which will be for the healing of the nations (Rev. 22:1-3). The Feast of Tabernacles is a rehearsal for the millennial reign of the Messiah and the ultimate recreation of the heavens and the earth.

Second, this was a time when God Himself dwelt in the midst of their camp. During the years in the wilderness, the Tabernacle of God was literally right in the center of the camp. The pillar of cloud provided shelter during the day and the pillar of fire provided light during the night. When Jesus comes back, He will dwell in Jerusalem in the midst of the people. He will rule and reign with truth and righteousness. Isaiah describes Jerusalem after the final battle and restoration this way:

> Isaiah 4:5-6 MKJV And the LORD will create over all the site of Mount Zion, and on her assemblies, a cloud and smoke by day, and the shining of a flaming fire by night; for on all the glory shall be a defense. And there shall be a booth for a shade by day from the heat, and for a refuge, and for a hiding place from storm and rain.

This is a perfect description of the time Israel dwelt in the wilderness and God was in their midst.

This feast more than any others was to be observed with rejoicing. During the time of Jesus, the feast was a twenty-four hour a day seven day non-stop celebration. The temple was lit up with huge torches lighting up the entire countryside. Jerusalem was called the "Light of the World." Jesus, our "Light of the World" will come and be the light from Jerusalem. When the earth is recreated and the heavenly Jerusalem comes down to join heaven to earth, there will be no need for light from the sun or the moon (Rev 21:22-23).

As we rejoice during the feast, we look forward to the return of Messiah and the redeemed who go up to Zion. Isaiah says:

> Isaiah 51:11 MKJV "Therefore the redeemed of the LORD shall return and come with singing into Zion; and everlasting joy shall be on their head. Gladness and joy shall overtake them; sorrow and mourning shall flee away."

This will be a time of rejoicing such as never has been!

Let's rehearse the joyful time when Jesus our Messiah will begin His reign on earth. Let's look one thousand years beyond that to the new creation where death will be swallowed up in victory (1 Cor. 15:54).

Reason Two to Celebrate the Feast of Tabernacles

The Feast of Tabernacles is marked by special sacrificial offerings. Among them were fourteen male lambs each day. This number is two times seven. Seven again is the number for spiritual completion but two is the number of division. What is the division here? The answer is in the other sacrifices. There was a succession of bulls sacrificed starting with thirteen on the first day and ending with seven on the last day. This totals seventy bulls which just happens to be the number of the nations as they were determined after the Tower of Babel (Deut. 32:8). As they sacrificed the bulls, Israel was acting in her divinely appointed role of priests to the nations (Ex. 19:6). The division is between Israel and all the gentile nations. Israel has been separated out as God's portion among the nations (Deut. 32:9).

The Feast is observed after the harvest has been brought in (Ex. 23:16), after "you have gathered in the labors out of your field." Jesus said that we are the workers in the field; that we have a harvest to bring in (Matt. 9:37-38). He also has a final harvest that He will bring in (Rev. 14:14-20, Matt. 13:36-43). After the harvest, we have a huge party. The wedding supper of the Lamb is ready. Blessed are those invited to the wedding supper of the Lamb.

> Revelation 19:6-7 MKJV And I heard as the sound of a great multitude, and as the sound of many waters, and as the sound of strong thunders, saying, Hallelujah! For the Lord God omnipotent reigns! Let us be glad and rejoice and we will give glory to Him.

For the marriage of the Lamb has come, and His wife has prepared herself.

If this isn't enough, there are special observance every seventh year and every fiftieth year. The fiftieth year, of course, follows the seventh seven year period. Every seventh year is a Sabbath year; again we see the number of spiritual completion. Every fiftieth year is the Year of Jubilee (Lev. 25). In the year of Jubilee, prisoners are set free and land is returned to the family who originally owned it. Jesus proclaimed a Year of Jubilee when He began His ministry (Luke 4:18-21 quoting Is. 61). Jesus fulfilled the first part of this chapter in His first coming; He did not fulfill the part about the Day of Vengeance of our God (verse 2). This will be the harvest referred to as the winepress of His wrath (Is. 63:1-13). The grape harvest begins in late July and continues conveniently enough until right before the Feast of Tabernacles. The proclamation of the Year of Jubilee occurs on Yom Kippur or the Day of Atonement which occurs just five days before the Feast of Tabernacles. On the subsequent Feast of Tabernacles, everyone, men, women, children and the stranger, gathers in Jerusalem to hear the King read the Torah! (Deut. 31:10-13) One of the first acts of Jesus, who is the Living Word, will be to read His Written Word to all those He has gathered to Himself in Jerusalem.

Isaiah 2:3 MKJV And many people shall go and say, Come, and let us go to the mountain of the LORD, to the house of the God of Jacob. And He will teach us of His ways, and we will walk in His paths. For out of Zion shall go out the Law, and the word of the LORD from Jerusalem.

Reason Three to Celebrate the Feast of Tabernacles: The Last Great Day of the Feast

The Feast of Tabernacles lasts for seven days with the last day called "Hashanna Rabba" which means the Great Hosanna. Hosanna means "save now" so the last day is the "great save now" where the Israelites cry out to God for salvation.

Part of the ceremony of the Feast is the ritual of water pouring which developed out of the words of Isaiah 12:3, "And with joy you shall draw water out of the wells of salvation." The high priest carrying a golden pitcher, and his assistant carrying a silver pitcher with wine in it, went down to the pool of Siloam. Jewish pilgrims lined the road leading to the pool waving their lulavs, a bouquet of the four species they used in their rejoicing in the Feast (Lev. 23:40). With all the people watching, the high priest dipped his pitcher into the pool drawing out living water.

Living water is water that flows. It has a continual inflow and outflow. A cistern, for example, would not be living water. The pools for washing at the temple were designed to be constantly flowing. The pool of Siloam was fed by the spring Gihon and so was living water. The word Siloam means "Sent" and Gihon, which is the name of one of the rivers flowing out of the Garden of Eden, means "to gush or break forth, to labor to bring forth." The living water from the pool of Siloam can be seen as a symbol of Jesus. It breaks forth from the Garden of Eden sent to bring salvation.

The High priest and his assistant proceed ceremoniously back to the temple with the pitchers of water and wine where they will be met by another group of priests who had gone down to the valley east of Jerusalem and cut thirty feet tall willow branches. The two groups meet in the temple around the altar. The High priest and his assistant proceed up the ramp to the altar while the other priests march around the altar with their willow branches. The people join in around them waving their lulavs. All are singing a combination of Isaiah 12:3, the song of Moses from Exodus 15:1-2, and the Hallelujah Psalms, Psalms 113-118. They finish with Psalm 118.

> Psalms 118:25-29 KJV Save now, I beseech thee, O LORD: O LORD, I beseech thee, send now prosperity. Blessed be he that cometh in the name of the LORD: we have blessed you out of the house of the LORD. God is the LORD, which hath shewed us light: bind the sacrifice with cords, even unto the horns of the altar. Thou art my God, and I will praise thee: thou art my God, I will exalt thee. O give thanks unto the LORD; for he is good: for his mercy endureth for ever.

As they sing the final verse, the people lift their lulavs and wave them toward the altar. This ceremony was conducted each day of the feast. On each of the first six days, the priests circled the altar only once. On the last great day, they circled seven times. It is at this time on the great day of the Feast as the worshippers completed their final circuit of the altar in the pause at the end of the song that "Jesus stood and cried, saying, 'If any man thirst, let him come unto me, and drink. He that believeth on me, as the scripture hath said, out of his belly shall flow rivers of living water'" (John 7:37-38).

The Israelites recognized this as a Messianic claim. Ezekiel writes of a river of living water flowing from the temple in the days of Messiah (Eze. 47). Zechariah writes of Living water flowing from Jerusalem in the days of Messiah (Zech. 14). Jeremiah says that the LORD Himself is a fountain of living water.

> Jeremiah 17:13 KJV O LORD, the hope of Israel, all that forsake thee shall be ashamed, and they that depart from me shall be written in the earth, because they have forsaken the LORD, the fountain of living waters.

On this great day of the Feast, what were the reactions of the Israelites? John tells us that some believed He was the Christ, the Messiah. Others didn't know what to believe. They would have six months before Passover to make their decisions.

When Jesus came into Jerusalem on the tenth of Nisan, four days before Passover, He was greeted with pilgrims lining the streets waving palm branches before Him, shouting "Blessed is He who comes in the name of the LORD, Hosanna, Blessed is the King of Israel." Waving palm branches was not something that was done at Passover. Remember those lulavs from the Feast of Tabernacles? They were made up of willow, myrtle and palm branches and the citron fruit. The willow and the myrtle would not yet have leaves at the time of Passover but the Palm tree would. Their greeting of Jesus at this time was more like the ceremony of water pouring at the Feast of Tabernacles! Further, the sages say that one of the reasons they were to rejoice with lulavs was to remember that even creation recognizes and praises God.

Luke records that during this triumphant entry into Jerusalem that some of the Pharisees cried out for Jesus to rebuke his disciples. What was Jesus' response?

Luke 19:40 KJV And he answered and said unto them, I tell you that, if these should hold their peace, the stones would immediately cry out.

On a future Feast of Tabernacles, the words of Ezekiel and Jeremiah will come true; living water will flow from the temple in Jerusalem.

Ezekiel 47:12 NASB "And by the river on its bank, on one side and on the other, will grow all kinds of trees for food. Their leaves will not wither, and their fruit will not fail. They will bear every month because their water flows from the sanctuary, and their fruit will be for food and their leaves for healing."

The stones that were silent when Jesus entered Jerusalem for that fateful Passover won't be silent then. All creation will burst out in praise!

Isaiah 44:23 MKJV Sing, O heavens; for the LORD has done it. Shout, lower parts of the earth. Break out into singing, O mountains, O forest, and every tree in it. For the LORD has redeemed Jacob, and glorified Himself in Israel.

Reasons to Celebrate the Feast of Tabernacles: Shimeni Atzerat—the Eighth Day Assembly

Although the Feast of Tabernacles is seven days long, the eighth day, the day after the feast, is to be observed with a holy convocation or assembly.

> Le 23:36 MKJV Seven days you shall offer a fire offering to the LORD. On the eighth day shall be a holy convocation to you. And you shall offer a fire offering to the LORD. It is a solemn assembly. And you shall do no work of labor.

The scripture doesn't offer any obvious clues as to the nature of the assembly only that it is to be held on the eighth day. What is the significance of the eighth day? The number eight represents new beginnings. What new beginning is being observed on this day? Each year, this eighth day, called Shimeni Atzerat, begins a new feast cycle. This cycle will repeat each year until Jesus comes again. When He does come, this day begins the millennial reign of Jesus. Let's look at what Zechariah said will occur every year of Jesus' reign.

> Zec 14:16 MKJV And it shall be, everyone who is left of all the nations which came up against Jerusalem shall go up from year to year to worship the King, the LORD of hosts, and to keep the Feast of Tabernacles.

Also in nearly identical words in Micah and Isaiah:

Mic 4:2 MKJV And many nations shall come and say, Come and let us go up to the mountain of the LORD, and to the house of the God of Jacob. And He will teach us of His ways, and we will walk in His paths; for the law shall go forth out of Zion, and the word of the LORD from Jerusalem.

Isa 2:3 MKJV And many people shall go and say, Come, and let us go to the mountain of the LORD, to the house of the God of Jacob. And He will teach us of His ways, and we will walk in His paths. For out of Zion shall go out the Law, and the word of the LORD from Jerusalem.

Scripture clearly connects observing the Feast of Tabernacles with the teaching of Torah and so, Shimeni Atzerat is also called Simchat Torah or Rejoice in the Torah. Each year, the Books of Moses are read through. Shimeni Atzerat marks the new beginning of reading the Torah. The book of Deuteronomy is finished and Genesis started again without a break. It is customary to stay up all night studying the Torah. Jesus Himself will teach Torah to all nations in the millennium.

Isa 54:13 MKJV And all your sons shall be taught of the LORD; and great shall be the peace of your sons.

We can celebrate Shimeni Atzerat as we keep in mind the words of Paul in 2 Timothy:

2 Timothy 3:16-17 MKJV All Scripture is God-breathed, and is profitable for doctrine, for reproof, for correction, for instruction in righteousness, that the man of God may be perfected, thoroughly furnished to every good work.

Let us spend the day in study as we look forward to the return of the Messiah, the author and finisher of our faith.

One thousand years later, there will be another Feast of Tabernacles which establishes the new heaven and earth, and the reign of God and the Lamb forever.

Re 22:1-5 MKJV And he showed me a pure river of water of life, clear as crystal, proceeding out of the throne of God and of the Lamb. In the midst of its street, and of the river, from here and from there, was the Tree of Life, which bore twelve fruits, each yielding its fruit according to one month. And the leaves of the tree were for the healing of the nations. And every curse will no longer be; but the throne of God and of the Lamb will be in it, and His servants will serve Him. And they will see His face, and His name will be in their foreheads. And there will be no night there. And they need no lamp, or light of the sun; for the Lord God gives them light. And they will reign forever and ever.

The Sabbath

Six days shall work be done, but the seventh day is the sabbath of rest, a holy convocation. You shall not do any work. It is a sabbath to the LORD in all your dwellings.
(Leviticus 23:3 MKJV)

Reasons to Celebrate the Sabbath

Many people don't think of the Sabbath as being a Biblical feast, but it is actually the first feast that God mentions in His list of feasts in Leviticus.

> Leviticus 23:2-3 MKJV Speak to the sons of Israel and say to them, The feasts of the LORD, which you shall proclaim, holy convocations, even these are My appointed feasts. Six days shall work be done, but the seventh day is the sabbath of rest, a holy convocation. You shall not do any work. It is a sabbath to the LORD in all your dwellings.

The Sabbath is a feast, an appointed time, on which God promises to meet with His people. He established this precedent long before the time of Moses. On the seventh day of creation, God rested and set the pattern for all generations.

> Genesis 2:2-3 MKJV And on the seventh day God ended His work which He had made. And He rested on the seventh day from all His work which He had made. And God blessed the seventh day and sanctified it, because in it He had rested from all His work which God created to make.

The word "sanctify" in this passage means to set apart. God set this day apart from the other six days of the week. In what ways are we to treat this day differently from other days?

During the six days of creation, God continually refers to His work as good. We can celebrate the Sabbath by reflecting on God's work and praising Him as the creator and king of the universe.

The passage in Genesis also tells us that God Himself rested. The word for rested is the Hebrew word shabath from which we get Sabbath. It means to cease from exertion. The number seven is the number of spiritual completion. God's rest on the seventh day of creation also looks forward to the completion of His plan of redemption.

> Hebrews 4:9-11 MKJV So then there remains a rest to the people of God. For he who has entered into his rest, he also has ceased from his own works, as God did from His. Therefore let us labor to enter into that rest, lest anyone fall after the same example of unbelief.

We can celebrate the Sabbath by resting in His salvation recognizing that none of our good works can bring salvation (Eph. 2:8-9). Symbolically, we put this into practice by ceasing our every day activities and spending the day focused on God and His son Jesus. It is a time of praise and thanksgiving. Isaiah tells us that taking delight in the Sabbath is the way to delight in God.

> Isaiah 58:13-14 NKJV "If you turn away your foot from the Sabbath, From doing your pleasure on My holy day, And call the Sabbath a delight, The holy day of the LORD honorable, And shall honor Him, not doing your own ways, Nor finding your own pleasure, Nor speaking your own words, Then you shall delight yourself in the LORD; And I will cause you to ride on the high hills of the earth, And feed

you with the heritage of Jacob your father. The mouth of the LORD has spoken."

It is a time to set aside our own desires and honor Him. Jesus spent His Sabbaths at the synagogues teaching God's word (Luke 4:16), in fellowship with His Jewish brothers (Luke 14:1), and in "doing good" (Matt. 12:10-12). We can come together and rejoice with our fellow believers and rest in the hope we have in Jesus our Messiah.

We can celebrate the Sabbath in joy as we look forward to the ultimate spiritual completion, Jesus' coming reign and the recreation of the heavens and the earth. At that time, we will have truly entered into God's rest.

> Revelation 21:3-5 NKJV And I heard a loud voice from heaven saying, "Behold, the tabernacle of God is with men, and He will dwell with them, and they shall be His people. God Himself will be with them and be their God. "And God will wipe away every tear from their eyes; there shall be no more death, nor sorrow, nor crying. There shall be no more pain, for the former things have passed away." Then He who sat on the throne said, "Behold, I make all things new." And He said to me, "Write, for these words are true and faithful."

The Feast of Purim

The story of the queen who saved her people

And Mordecai wrote these things, and sent letters to all the Jews in all the provinces of the king Ahasuerus, near and far, to establish among them that they should keep the fourteenth day of the month Adar, and the fifteenth day of the same, yearly, as the days in which the Jews rested from their enemies, and the month which was turned to them from sorrow to joy, and from mourning into a good day that they should make them days of feasting and joy, and of sending portions to one another, and gifts to the poor.

(Esther 9:20-22 MKJV)

Reasons to Celebrate Purim

Purim is the holiday that is established in the book of Esther. It is celebrated in the late winter or early spring one month before Passover. It commemorates the defeat of Haman, the enemy of the Jews.

> Esther 9:27-28 MKJV the Jews ordained, and took on them and on their seed, and on all such as joined themselves to them, so as it should not fail, that they would keep these two days according to their writing, and according to their time every year and that these days should be remembered and kept throughout every generation, every family, every province, and every city and these days of Purim should not fail from among the Jews, nor the memorial of them perish from their seed.

Haman was an Amalekite, a descendant of Jacob's brother Esau. The Amalekites harbored a hatred for Israel from the time Israel first came up out of Egypt. The first battle the Irsaelites fought was against the Amalekites. God pronounced judgment against Amalek for the way they attacked Israel (Ex. 17:8-16).

Haman, following in the path of his ancestors, plotted to have all the Jews killed.

> Esther 3:5-6 MKJV And when Haman saw that Mordecai did not bow nor worship him, then Haman was full of wrath. And he scorned to lay hands only on Mordecai, for they had revealed to him the people

of Mordecai. And Haman sought to destroy all the Jews throughout the whole kingdom of Ahasuerus, the people of Mordecai.

The unreasoning hatred of Haman reminds us of the hatred and persecution suffered by the Jewish people through the centuries, many times at the instigation of the church. Christians can celebrate Purim as a means to repent of the actions of our church fathers towards the Jewish people. The prophet Daniel is a model for this repentance. When Daniel knew that the 70 years of exile for Judah were coming to an end, he repented of the acts of his fathers.

> Daniel 9:4-6 MKJV And I prayed to the LORD my God, and made my confession, and said, O Lord, the great and awesome God, keeping the covenant and mercy to those who love Him, and to those who keep His commandments, we have sinned and have committed iniquity, and have done wickedly, and have rebelled, even by departing from Your commandments and from Your judgments. Neither have we listened to Your servants the prophets, who spoke in Your name to our kings, our rulers, and our fathers, and to all the people of the land.

Even though Daniel himself was a great man of God, he did not consider himself separate from his fellow Israelites or unaccountable for the acts of his forefathers. As the time of Jesus' second coming approaches, we as Christians need to confess the sins of our Christian forefathers and return to our God, the same God who is the God of Israel and all the prophets.

The outcome of Haman's plotting was not what he expected. Queen Esther, herself a Jew although Haman did not know it, exposed his plot. Haman and his ten sons were hanged on the very gallows he had erected to kill Mordecai. The Jewish people were then given permission to kill those who would try to kill them on the day Haman decreed should be the day of their execution. On that day, the Jewish people fought back and won a great victory. Once again, the nations will gather against Israel to destroy her. Jesus, a Jew although many Christians don't seem to know it, will reveal the plot against Israel and bring them to justice.

> Joel 3:1-3 MKJV For, behold, in those days and in that time, when I will bring again the exiles of Judah and Jerusalem, I will also gather all nations and will bring them down into the valley of Jehoshaphat. And I will fight with them there for My people and for My inheritance Israel, whom they have scattered among the nations, and **divided My land**. And they have cast lots for My people, and have given a boy for a prostitute, and sold a girl for wine, so that they might drink.

Like Haman, the nations plot and cast lots (Purim) for the destruction of God's people. Even now, our own nation is pressuring Israel to divide God's land. In Esther's time as the day of the decree approached, many people began to fear God and joined themselves to the Jewish people.

> Esther 8:17 MKJV And in every province, and in every city where the king's command and his order came, the Jews had joy and gladness, a feast and a good day. And many of the people of the land became Jews, for the fear of the Jews fell on them.

Christians can celebrate Purim as a sign of solidarity with the Jewish people. The outcome of the battle when the nations come against Jerusalem will have the same outcome as the battle in the days of Esther.

> Joel 3:11-14 MKJV Gather yourselves and come, all you nations, and gather yourselves together all around; cause Your mighty ones to come down there, O LORD. Let the nations be awakened and come up to the valley of Jehoshaphat; for there I will sit to judge all the nations all around. Put in the sickle, for the harvest is ripe. Come, come down; for the press is full; the vats overflow, for their wickedness is great. Multitudes, multitudes in the valley of decision; for the day of the LORD is near in the valley of decision!

In the final verse of the book of Esther, we read that Mordecai ruled second only to King Ahasuerus seeking justice and peace for his people.

> Esther 10:3 YLT For Mordecai the Jew is second to king Ahasuerus, and a great man of the Jews, and accepted of the multitude of his brethren, seeking good for his people, and speaking peace to all his seed.

The book of Chronicles records the same about David's reign.

> 1 Chronicles 18:14 KJV So David reigned over all Israel, and executed judgment and justice among all his people.

When Jesus comes again, he will save Judah just like Mordecai and Esther, and He will rule second only to God with peace and justice.

Jeremiah 33:15-16 MKJV In those days, and at that time, I will cause the Branch of righteousness to grow up to David. And He shall do judgment and righteousness in the land. In those days Judah shall be saved, and Jerusalem shall dwell safely. And this is the name with which she shall be called, THE LORD OUR RIGHTEOUSNESS.

Isn't it time for those who call themselves by the name of Jesus Christ, Yeshua the Messiah of Israel, to stand with Israel?

The Feast of Hanukkah

Rededication and renewal

And the Feast of Dedication took place at Jerusalem, and it was winter.

(John 10:22 MKJV)

Reason One to Celebrate Hanukkah

The first reason to celebrate Hanukkah is that Jesus celebrated Hanukkah. His observance is recorded in the book of John. The word Hanukkah means dedication and its observance is in December.

> John 10:22-23 KJV And it was at Jerusalem the feast of the dedication, and it was winter. 23 And Jesus walked in the temple in Solomon's porch.

Much of Jesus' ministry was in the area around the Sea of Galilee with only occasional visits to Jerusalem. John records Jesus in Jerusalem only at the Feasts of the LORD. Yet John records this visit to Jerusalem that is not on one of the Feasts ordained by God in Leviticus 23. What is special about this particular Hanukkah?

First, it follows the very eventful Feast of Tabernacles during which Jesus stood in the middle of the Ceremony of Water Pouring and declared that He was the Living Water (John 7:37-38). The temple guards who were appointed to arrest Him came back empty-handed declaring that no one ever spoke the way He did (John 7:45-46). Jesus said He was the Light of the World (John 8:12), declared that He existed before Abraham (John 8:58), and healed a man born blind (John 9:1-12). He said He was the Good Shepherd spoken of by Isaiah (Isaiah 40:11) and Ezekiel (Ezekiel 34). As a result, many believed He was the Messiah and many did not (John 10:19-21).

The following spring, Jesus would again go to Jerusalem; this time to die as the Passover Lamb that would take away the sins of the world. He would fulfill His words spoken during that eventful Feast of Tabernacles that He was indeed the Good Shepherd who would lay down His life for His sheep (John 10:14-18).

So, what is Jesus teaching during Hanukkah? What message is He trying to communicate? The Jewish people of Jerusalem come to Him and ask, "Are you the one?" Since this is Hanukkah, thoughts of the great hero Judah Maccabeus must have been foremost on their minds. "Are you the Messiah who will deliver us from Rome like Judah Maccabeus delivered us from Antiochus IV Epiphanes?" Jesus continues His teaching from the Feast of Tabernacles, "I am the Good Shepherd." He is not coming at this time in the manner of a Judah Maccabeus.

> John 10:25-29 MKJV Jesus answered them, I told you and you did not believe. The works that I do in My Father's name, they bear witness of Me. But you did not believe because you are not of My sheep. As I said to you, My sheep hear My voice, and I know them, and they follow Me. And I give to them eternal life, and they shall never ever perish, and not anyone shall pluck them out of My hand. My Father who gave them to me is greater than all, and no one is able to pluck them out of My Father's hand.

Sadly, many of Jesus' questioners reject His words and conclude that He is not the Messiah.

> John 10:31-33 MKJV Then the Jews took up stones again to stone Him. Jesus answered them, I have shown you many good works from My Father; for

which of these do you stone Me? The Jews answered Him, saying, We do not stone you for a good work, but for blasphemy, and because you, being a man, make yourself God.

But Jesus is reaching out one last time to those who will hear His voice and come to Him for everlasting life.

John 10:37-38 MKJV If I do not do the works of My Father, do not believe Me. But if I do, though you do not believe Me, believe the works so that you may know and believe that the Father is in Me, and I in Him.

Afterwards, Jesus leaves Jerusalem and goes to the same place where John baptized across the Jordan. Jesus goes back to where His ministry began and many came to Him there.

John 10:40-42 MKJV And He went away again beyond Jordan into the place where John baptized at the first, and He stayed there. And many came to Him and said, John indeed did no miracle, but all things that John said concerning this One were true. And many believed on Him there.

Their belief in Him would be tested that very spring at Passover. Who will they say He is then?

Hanukah celebrates the rededication of the temple after it was desecrated by Antiochus IV Epiphanes. Jewish tradition says that there was not enough holy oil to keep the temple menorah lit for the eight days needed for the rededication of the temple. They lit the menorah anyway and the oil lasted through all eight days until new oil could be made and consecrated. The special nine-branched Hanukkiah is lit to declare the miracles of Hanukah—both the miraculous victories through Judah Maccabeus and of the oil.

Christians can light the Hanukkiah as a rededication of their own lives as the living temple of God, to live a life of holiness.

> 1 Corinthians 3:16-17 MKJV Do you not know that you are a temple of God, and that the Spirit of God dwells in you? If anyone defiles the temple of God, God shall destroy him. For the temple of God is holy, which you are.

Christians can light the Hanukkiah to celebrate the miracle of new birth displaying the light for all to see. Just like Jesus told his questioners to examine the works He does and see if they are from the father, we too need to do the good works the father gives us to do.

> Matthew 5:16 MKJV Let your light so shine before men that they may see your good works and glorify your Father who is in Heaven.

As we celebrate Hanukkah, who do you say He is?

Reason Two to Celebrate Hanukkah

The events commemorated by Hanukah are the fulfillment of prophecy. Daniel prophesies about the rise of the Greek empire by Alexander the Great, Alexander's early death, and the dividing of his kingdom into four separate kingdoms each led by one of his generals.

> Daniel 8:19-22 MKJV And he said, Behold, I will make you know what shall happen in the last end of the indignation. For it is for the time appointed for the end. The ram which you saw having two horns are the kings of Media and Persia. And the shaggy goat is the king of Greece. And the great horn between his eyes is the first king. And as for that being broken, and four stood up in its place; four kingdoms shall stand up out of the nation, but not in its power.

Two of the four kingdoms are of interest prophetically. These are the Seleucid and Ptolemaic kingdoms. General Seleucus and the kingdom he establishes becomes the king of the north in Daniel chapter 11. This kingdom consists of Syria, the heart of the old Babylonian and Assyrian Empires, and parts of Asia Minor. General Ptolemy and his successors become the king of the south. The kingdom of the south consists of the greater Egyptian region and parts of Asia Minor. These two kingdoms will fight over and through the land of Israel from the death of Alexander in 323 B.C. to the death of Antiochus IV Epiphanes in 163

B.C. Daniel chapter 11 chronicles the back and forth relationship between these two kingdoms.[1]

The following list gives the verse in Daniel 11 followed by the King of the North and the King of the South referenced in the verse.

Daniel 11

1. verse 5: Seleucus I Nacator (312 to 281 B.C.) Ptolemy I Soter (323-285 B.C.)

2. Not referenced: Antiochus I Soter (281-262 B.C.) Ptolemy II (285-246 B.C.)

3. verse 6: Antiochus II Theos (262-246 B.C.) Ptolemy II

4. verses 7-9: Seleucus II Callinicus (246-227B.C.) Ptolemy III (246-221 B.C.)

5. verse 10: Seleucus III Soter (227-223 B.C.) Ptolemy III

6. verses 10-11, 13: Antiochus III the Great (223-187 B.C.) Ptolemy IV

7. verses 15-19: Antiochus III Ptolemy V

8. verse 20: Seleucus IV Philopater

9. verses 21-32: Antiochus IV Epiphanes Ptolemy Philopater

---

[1] Moore, Beth, Daniel: lives of Integrity Words of Prophecy; Lifeway Press, Nashville, Tennessee, 2006

The Ptolemies started out with control of Israel. They were lenient rulers allowing those under their rule to practice their own religion without interference. However the Seleucids were intent on "civilizing" or Hellenizing those under their rule. They pushed the worship of the Greek gods and renamed cities to reflect the new regime. Antiochus III the Great drove the Ptolemies out of Israel and began the Hellenizing process of Israel. It was Antiochus IV Epiphanes, however, who issued an edict forbidding the worship of any but the Greek gods. As you can imagine, this did not sit well with most of the Israelites. Needless to say, the province of Israel was not highly regarded by Antiochus.

After one of his forays against Egypt, while returning to his own land, he plundered the Temple of God.

> Daniel 11:28 MKJV And he shall return to his land with great riches. And his heart shall be against the holy covenant. And he will act, and he shall return to his land.

Two years later, he again attacks Egypt. When it appears that he will finally triumph against Egypt, Rome steps in and gives him a choice to return to his own land or face the power of Rome. Enraged, he returns to his land. This time when he goes through Israel, he murders 80,000 people with the help of the Jews who have been Hellenized. He sets up an altar to Zeus over God's altar. This is called the abomination of desolation.

> Daniel 11:29-31 MKJV At the time appointed he shall return and come against the south. But it shall not be as the former or as the latter. For the ships of Kittim shall come against him. And he shall be grieved and return, and have fury against the holy

covenant. So he shall do; he shall even return and give heed to those who forsake the holy covenant. And forces will stand from him, and they will profane the sanctuary, the fortress, and shall remove the daily sacrifice, and they shall place the desolating abomination.

The family of Mattathias, a priest from Modein, rises up against Antiochus and his generals. Mattathias' son Judah leads the battles against Antiochus' forces. They win time after time against overwhelming odds. The defeat of Antiochus' forces at the hands of Israel brought about the decline and fall of the Seleucid Empire.

Daniel 11:32 NKJV "Those who do wickedly against the covenant he shall corrupt with flattery; but the people who know their God shall be strong, and carry out great exploits.

Hanukkah commemorates Israel's victory over Antiochus IV Epiphanes and the rededication of the second temple. The Hanukkiah is lit after dark and placed in a window or even better on a porch where all who pass by can see it. It is a proclamation of the miracles God performed in driving the forces of Antiochus out of Israel and destroying the Seleucid Empire.

What miracles has God done in your life? What miracles on the scale of the battles against Antiochus IV Epiphanes will God again do at the time of the end? We can light the candles of the Hanukkiah to remember what God has done in each of our lives, chief of which is bringing us into His glorious Light.

John 12:46 NKJV "I have come as a light into the world, that whoever believes in Me should not abide in darkness.

We can light the candles of the Hanukkiah in anticipation of when Jesus will return bringing light into the darkness once more.

Revelation 21:23 NKJV The city had no need of the sun or of the moon to shine in it, for the glory of God illuminated it. The Lamb is its light.

Reason Three to Celebrate Hanukkah

The third reason to celebrate Hanukkah is that the events commemorated by Hanukkah are spoken of by Jesus as having future prophetic significance. The words He speaks to His disciples telling them of the signs of His coming and the end of the world resound with Hanukkah language. First, Jesus speaks of another abomination of desolation. Then He goes on to invoke images of the horror inflicted on the Jewish people during the reign of Antiochus IV Epiphanes.

> Matthew 24:15-21 MKJV Therefore when you see the abomination of desolation, spoken of by Daniel the prophet, stand in the holy place (whoever reads, let him understand). Then let those in Judea flee into the mountains. Let him on the housetop not come down to take anything out of his house; nor let him in the field turn back to take his clothes. And woe to those who are with child, and to those who give suck in those days! But pray that your flight is not in the winter, nor on the sabbath day; for then shall be great tribulation, such as has not been since the beginning of the world to this time; no, nor ever shall be.

Antiochus set up an altar to Zeus over the altar of God in the Temple. The two books of Maccabbees are not included in the scriptures but they describe the events of that time.

> I Maccabees 1:57-59, 62 On the fifteenth day of Chislev in the year one hundred and forty-five

(December 8, 167 B.C.) the king erected the abomination of desolation above the altar; and altars were built in the surrounding towns of Judah and incense offered at the doors of houses and in the streets. On the twenty-fifth of the month sacrifice was offered on the altar erected over the altar of holocaust.

Those in Judea fled into the wilderness taking most of their possessions with them. They were pursued and attacked on the Sabbath.

1 Maccabees 2:29-30, 32, 38 At this many who were concerned for virtue and justice went down to the desert and stayed there, taking with them their sons, their wives and their cattle, for the burden of their wrongs had become unendurable. A strong detachment went after them, and when it came up with them ranged itself against them in battle formation, preparing to attack them on the Sabbath day. The attack was pressed home on the Sabbath itself, and they were slaughtered with their wives and children and cattle, to the number of one thousand persons.

Those in Jerusalem didn't fare any better. In fact the slaughter there was even worse.

2 Maccabees 5:24-27 The king also sent the mysarch Appolonius at the head of an army twenty-two thousand strong, with orders to put to death all men in their prime and to sell the women and children. Arriving in Jerusalem and posing as a man of peace, this man waited until the holy day of the Sabbath and then, taking advantage of the Jews as they rested

from work, ordered his men to parade fully armed; all those who came out to watch he put to the sword; then running through the city with his armed troops, he cut down an immense number of people.

Josephus writes that ten thousand women and children were sold into slavery on that day and the temple was totally plundered of all its wealth. Those who resisted by reading or even having a Torah scroll, by observing the Sabbath, or circumcising their sons died a horrific death. This was especially true of women who circumcised their babies. Josephus records in The Antiquities of the Jews, Book 12, Chapter 5, line 256:

> "...for they were whipped with rods and their bodies were torn to pieces, and were crucified while they were still alive and breathed; they also strangled those women and their sons whom they had circumcised, as the king had appointed, hanging their sons about their necks as they were upon the crosses."

The words of Jesus in Matthew 24 match that day in December exactly. The abomination of desolation was set up in the temple in the winter. The people were brutally attacked on the Sabbath more than once. And woe to the women! Those who circumcised their infant sons died grievous deaths. As horrible as those days were, Jesus said the days leading up to His return would be even worse. He warns His listeners not to try to bring their possessions with them but to flee immediately. He says that **THEN** shall be great tribulation worse than has ever been seen before. The events of December 167 B.C. foreshadow the events of the great tribulation. Antiochus IV Epiphanes is a shadow of the Antichrist. His reign name of Epiphanes means "God

Manifest." Paul tells us that the Antichrist will set himself up as God.

> 2 Thessalonians 2:3-4 MKJV Let not anyone deceive you by any means. For that Day shall not come unless there first comes a falling away, and the man of sin shall be revealed, the son of perdition, who opposes and exalts himself above all that is called God, or that is worshiped, so that he sits as God in the temple of God, setting himself forth, that he is God.

Judah Maccabeus is a shadow of Jesus. Jesus is of the line of David of the tribe of Judah. Jacob's blessing over Judah includes describing him as a lion.

> Genesis 49:9 MKJV Judah is a lion's whelp. My son, you have gone up from the prey. He stooped, he crouched like a lion; and like a lioness, who shall rouse him?

Judah Maccabeus is described similarly in I Maccabees.

> I Macabbees 3: 3-4 He extended the fame of his people. He put on the breastplate like a giant and girded on his war harness; he engaged in battle after battle, protecting the ranks with his sword. He was like a lion's whelp roaring over its prey.

Jesus is a priest on the order of Melchizedek. Judah Maccabeus is a priest of the line of Aaron. Judah ruled over Israel at the time of the rededication of the temple. Jesus will rule over Israel and the whole world. He is the one who will build the third temple of God.

We can celebrate Hanukkah as we look forward to Jesus' return, learning, and watching so that we are not caught sleeping or unaware. We light the Hanukkiah to remind us that we are of the light and need to keep watch for the signs of His coming.

> 1 Thessalonians 5:4-6 MKJV But you, brothers, are not in darkness, that the Day should overtake you like a thief. You are all the sons of light and the sons of the day. We are not of the night, or of darkness. Therefore let us not sleep as the rest do, but let us watch and be calm.